LIFE ON THE PERIPHERY

LIFE ON THE PERIPHERY

AN ORDINARY MAN'S VIEW OF THE WORLD

BY LOUIS BRUNO

NO CEILING BOOKS · RONKONKOMA

Life on the Periphery
An Ordinary Man's View of the World

By Louis Bruno

Published by
No Ceiling Books
2519 Chestnut Avenue
Ronkonkoma, New York 11779

www.NoCeilingBooks.com
info@NoCeilingBooks.com

ISBN: 978-0-9911883-0-7 (trade paperback)
ISBN: 978-0-9911883-1-4 (e-book)

Design and composition: www.dmargulis.com

MANUFACTURED IN THE UNITED STATES OF AMERICA

CONTENTS

PREFACE

STARTED THREATENING TO write a book
when I was eighteen. My college roommate Mike
and I were talking late one night, and the idea
just came to me. I've always had a lot of thoughts,
ideas and opinions on everything from Babe Ruth to
the nervous system of the newt. This is not to imply
that any of my ramblings have any validity, but a man
must listen to his own ramblings even if nobody else
will. I told Mike that "someday" I'd write a book that
contained all my silly ideas. I've noticed that people
usually preface their goals with "someday." My aunt
often says "Someday, I'll get to Europe." Someday really means that you'll never really do it, but you are
reserving the right to visit this dream at a later date.
But I'm making good on my someday (even though no
one really cares).

The few people I've shared my book-writing dream
with were curious about the title. One explanation I
offer is that I can't think of a good or exciting title.

I love to observe life and people—and everything
in between. I've always considered myself an outsider.

PERIPHERY

This word has a negative connotation, but I'm using it in a positive way. I've always lived outside the system. I'm usually not in the inner circle or in the know. I often stay to myself and follow my own path, trying not to interfere with anyone else's path and expecting the same in return.

I'm an individualist. I'm neither a leader nor a follower. If I tried to lead, no one would follow. And if I tried to follow, I wouldn't listen. I put all my energy and attention into the things I truly love: my family, my friends, my work (I had to throw that one in just in case this book doesn't move off the shelf), and playing and watching sports.

I run into people all the time who seem to be experts on all subjects. They know the best place for Chinese food and pizza, the best doctor, lawyer, mechanic and barber. They understand global warming, the economy, politics and Shakespeare. If they were on a game show, their subject would be everything. This is not to imply that these individuals do not have a working knowledge of all of these subjects. In fact, I am quite certain that these folks, who have dead-end jobs and are constantly in a state of financial woe, are well versed in all of life's nuances.

On the other hand, I am just trying to make it through the week without wearing my underwear on the outside of my pants. My goal is to try to constrain my thoughts to the things I know, but we are all different. I do get involved in some meaningful endeavors, but sometimes I just dip my toe into the pool while others go in up to their neck. Sometimes I get mad at myself because I cherish my quiet time so much; I have to push myself to get involved in things more deeply and to create new experiences for myself. At 44, I'm still a work in progress. But I love to observe from afar, from the periphery.

If you visit a bookstore, you'll notice that any book there that deals with observations, thoughts, opinions, or ideas about life and all its nuances is either written by some type of doctor, psychologist, psychiatrist, or therapist or by a celebrity. I belong to none of these categories (as anyone who knows me can attest). I don't think we give ourselves enough credit. We're forever seeking solutions and advice externally. Books, tapes, seminars, you name it, we've tried it. This is not to dismiss or demean the necessity of these media in our culture. They are important and helpful. But we never look inward first. This external advice should not be used as a substitute for our ability to first help ourselves.

Also, we turn almost exclusively to external sources for our entertainment. Please don't misunderstand me. I love television, and I know lines from *The Honeymooners* better than the original cast. But television and movies have dulled our senses to a degree and have taken the place of our ability to amuse ourselves (for those with a dirty mind: please refrain from commenting).

As I approach my mid 40s and my children continue to grow and mature, I thought now would be a good time to fulfill my book writing dream (also I need the money). I realize that I am not well known, nor do I have an MD, PhD, DDS or any other letters after my name, but I have had thoughts, observations, and experiences (I figure that a regular guy like me is as entitled to these as Oprah, Dr. Phil, or the ladies on *The View*).

I hope you will see a lot of yourself in this book and be able to relate to my experiences, ideas, and opinions. Those of us who wake up early five or six days a week, battle traffic, and fight the daily grind only to wind up even or slightly behind rarely take a chance. Well, I'm giving it a shot and hoping for the best. "I couldn't" is a lot better to reminisce about than "I should've" or "I didn't." I have always loved observing people and their behavioral patterns, and I love to write, so I surmised that this would be a perfect combination. Anyway, what do I have to lose, besides my pride, dignity, self-respect, money, and future? Most people don't think I have much of a chance at any of these anyway. The point is that we all have thoughts, ideas, opines, views, observations and experiences. I'd love to share mine with you.

OPENING THOUGHTS

SOMETIMES I FEEL overwhelmed by the pressures, struggles, and responsibilities of life. You know these worries—the safety and wellbeing of our families, paying our mortgage, car payments, car insurance, car repairs (are you beginning to sense a common theme?), paying for our children's education, health care, caring for our elders, and so on. Let's not forget the oldies but goodies such as national security, the war on terror, crime, the environment—the list goes on and on.

But I have noticed that some other worries, which might be new worries or variations on old worries, have begun to penetrate our thoughts. I mean our collapse in confidence in our leaders and institutions. We have begun to show distrust, bitterness, anger, and cynicism toward these entities. My parents' generation had more faith and respect in this area. I don't know if it was blind faith or lack of knowledge or information, but we used to have more faith in our leaders and our institutions.

Technological advancement has led to our society being bombarded with immediate news and information that affects every area of our life. We no longer have the luxury of innocence or naiveté regarding the political world, the business world, the sports world, the religious world, and the like. It is impossible to pick up a newspaper (I realize I am showing my age as no member of our society under 30 reads a newspaper and no member of our society under 20 knows what a newspaper is).... What I meant to say is that it is impossible to check our phones, computers, or tablets and not read a story about politicians using their office for personal profit and gain (I know that this revelation comes as a shock), corruption in school districts and on school boards, indiscretions in the world of finance, athletes involved with performance enhancing drugs, violence, drunk driving, and the list goes on and on. I often hear of people in my age bracket who "can't relate" to any of the contemporary movies or television programs because of the gratuitous violence and sex and an overall lack of compelling storylines and characters we care about. This is not to suggest that previous generations did not experience some of these same feelings about their problems at the time, but the information age has allowed us to see the warts more clearly and experience the problems on a closer and more visceral level.

Obviously, some of these issues have a generational feel to them. My parents' generation feels that the world started going the wrong way a long time ago, and they are worried about the path we are traveling as a society. My children's generation, like most young generations, does not analyze the big picture quite so skeptically, and realizes that I may not like their music or movies as my parents may not have enjoyed our music or movies. I have also noticed that younger people are not as taken aback by scandal, probably because they have seen so much of it that they assume it is the norm, which is a sad commentary and a disturbing trend. Hopefully, our kids' generation will not get so apathetic and desensitized to these problems that they forego the opportunity to effect change, but will instead work to eradicate some of these problems. They may have an advantage in that it is already being acknowledged that there are a myriad of problems to attack.

Every generation is concerned that the next generation will cause our society to decline into a state of moral decay (from Elvis Presley shaking his hips on the *Ed Sullivan Show* to Lady GaGa and beyond), but there is a different feel to our contemporary woes. I hate to sound like an old fart complaining that the music is too loud or that the kids have hit the ball into my yard again, but there does seem to be some merit in the notion that either our standards or our values have eroded in a fundamental way.

Oftentimes we accept less and forgive more, because we feel we have no other choice. But We the People, especially the middle class, are the backbone of America. Politicians count on us to vote for them, hoping that we ignore their scandals and their abuse of power. Our taxes are forever being raised while the level of services is not necessarily being raised. The sports industry (I am an enormous sports fan) and the entertainment industry rely on us to pay to watch their product on either the small or big screen or to pay handsomely to see a live event.

We should not follow blindly, like lambs being led to slaughter. We should ask tough questions and demand honest and forthright answers. Character and integrity should be demanded from our elected officials, business leaders, and sports and entertainment icons (I know that you are thinking that with this as a standard we would not have enough bodies to fill these positions). Ultimately we have the power to effect change. We should view this as a responsibility to take seriously, and an opportunity to leave the next generation with a world that is in better shape than it was when our generation inherited it.

Without ignoring the problems facing our society, I am encouraged by some of the changes, albeit sometimes small changes, that have begun to take place. The towns on Long Island have separate pickups for the recycling of bottles and cans and paper products. Supermarkets, even mainstream supermarkets, offer many environmentally friendly cleaning supplies, as well as meat and poultry from animals that are fed a cleaner, healthier, and hormone-free diet and are more humanely raised. Many companies are encouraging their customers to go paperless to save trees.

There is a lot of talk in the media and on the Internet about living a healthier lifestyle. We hear about diet and exercise; positive thinking and a life-affirming outlook, as an avenue to a more rewarding and fulfilling journey through life; and being motivated both personally and professionally to have a sense of purpose and fulfillment. The idea is that if we start small and try to enhance and improve our lives, we can then build a solid foundation from which we could become galvanized to make changes and improvements on a higher level, especially if we could mobilize and work in a cooperative and constructive fashion rather than in a divisive and destructive fashion.

People are being encouraged to have a voice, become involved, to have a sense of social responsibility. All the exercise programs and diet books and commercials, television programs like Dr. Oz and Dr. Phil that address health and well-being, the endless talk from the political left and political right about our country's direction, and the grass roots gatherings and movements attempting to shine a light on corporate greed are evidence that we know we have problems that need to be addressed and we are running short on time to solve them. Identifying problems is the first step in solving them, but we must move forward with diligence and a sense of purpose, rather than with finger pointing and gridlock and a "someone else will clean up this mess" mentality.

While we all go around and around on these big picture issues, we still derive the greatest joy from the little moments and special experiences, such as watching our children grow up and blossom, the love we have for our family and our friends, a warm summer day with a cool ocean breeze, or just simply thumbing through a photo album. (I'm sorry, as I am showing my age again. For the Young Guns, the over 40 demographic places our special photos on pages in an album, and then we will look at the album to reminisce about past vacations, birthday parties, and Christmas memories. I realize that the younger demographic takes 467 pictures every day with their cell phone and then puts them on Facebook or wherever so that the entire world can see special things like the rug on your bedroom floor or an ant resting on your mailbox.)

We exist to cherish the small things; in the end, those are the things that will put the biggest smile on your face and provide the most fuel for your soul. Those who appreciate the little pleasures and have a passion for life, a sense of purpose, compassion, humility, and a sense of humor will reap the rewards life has to offer. They will live on a higher plane and motivate and encourage those around them to approach life with the same zeal. They will possess a sense of accomplishment and inner peace, serenity and contentment (and a larger bank account—let's never leave that out of the equation).

CHAPTER 1

THE EARLY YEARS—AND VIEWS ON THE CONTEMPORARY FAMILY

I F THE LEADING cause of divorce is marriage, then the leading cause of childhood has to be parents. Don't get me wrong; the decision to become a parent is among the most important a person makes in their life (though not everyone decides— some receive the news as a surprise). My parents are a classic example of the mindset of those who grew up in the 1950s and raised a family in the 1970s and 1980s. The sacrifices they made and their commitment to parenting, no matter what the financial or emotional cost, are astounding. Every decision they made while my sister Sarah and I were growing up had our best interests as the uppermost thought in their mind, sometimes at the expense of their own financial or emotional wellbeing. They were devoted to the notion that we would not have to do without. They wanted to give us everything they didn't have growing up. Parents who grew up with modest means say this to explain why they are shoving everything they did not have down our throats. For the most part, their heart was in the right place, but sometimes the execution of their plan could be slightly off the mark.

When I became a parent, my appreciation for the sacrifices my parents made grew exponentially. However, my parental approach differs slightly. My wife, Michelle, and I have told our two daughters, Deborah and Krista, that they can freely and openly discuss any subject with us without fear of judgment or embarrassment. Hopefully, this will enable them to grow up with correct facts (assuming that my facts about sex are correct).

My parents were raised in an old-fashioned Catholic school amid children of immigrants. This environment strongly, and I am stressing strongly, influenced their childrearing beliefs. Subjects such as sexuality, homosexuality, teen pregnancy, and abortion were discussed as often as a Halley's Comet sighting. To this day, these subjects are pretty much off the table as far as my parents are concerned. You can take the kid out of the old neighborhood, but you can never take the old neighborhood out of the kid. Whether or not to put the house dressing on the side or directly on their salad is about as controversial and provocative as their conversations get.

When I reflect on them as parents and grandparents and even taking into account all of their warts and idiosyncrasies, I was very lucky to have parents who made me feel loved and cherished every day of my life. At the end of the day, that's pretty damn good.

The attitude toward parenting has changed as circumstances have made doing things the old way impractical. The 1980s brought with them new family structures resulting from an increase in divorce and subsequent remarriage. Single-parent families, step-children, and half-brothers and half-sisters became a big part of the American vocabulary, experience, and reality. Mothers started to flood the workplace as never before, leaving kids alone in the house until a parent came home from work. (I am very grateful that mothers went to work, as my wife earns considerably more than I do. Viva Gloria Steinem and Norma Rae. Sorry to show my age again. For the younger crowd, Viva Lady GaGa).

Many believe the influx of working moms was the beginning of the "breakdown of the American value system." I'm not sure that I agree with that, and I can see both sides of the argument. However, with a wife, mother, mother in law, two daughters, a sister, and two female dogs very close to me, discretion is the better part of valor. Anyway, my point is that with mothers out of the home for an extended period of time, things began to change. Gone were the days of dad coming home at six o'clock and dinner being served at 6:05, whether it was ready to be served or not. We were soon going to be moving away from the idea that dinner consisted of two parents and 2.3 children discussing their day, although much of the conversation seemed to center around dad's workplace experience. His struggles for upward mobility, respect, a raise, a longer lunch hour, a better parking space, and the key to the executive men's room were the focal point of the dinner conversation. By the time the children of this generation had their own kids, the dads would have to play a larger role around the house, in every capacity (my dad reached his zenith the day he made his own toast and poured his own glass of orange juice. He then retired from domestic duties on a high note).

The household dynamic that existed when virtually every mom was a stay-at-home mom is much more difficult to attain in our contemporary economy. More and more families eat on the go or on the run. Fast food, pizza, and Chinese food menus are part of the décor in many homes. With most children in one kind of after school activity or another, there just aren't enough hours in the day to put a lot of time and effort into a long, drawn out meal on a nightly basis. Families try to do as much together as they can, but times change and we have to change with the times and try to adapt to this evolution. We can all debate what is better for kids and what is worse for kids, but there is little argument that if your children are made to feel special and important; are able to feel your love and support; are given a sense of rights, responsibilities, and purpose; and feel they can come to you with both their dreams and their problems, both their successes and disappointments; that no matter how cold the world can be at times, there will always be a warm place in your arms; they will be equipped with the proper tools to take on life's battle, no matter what the odds (and let's face it, they will wind up living with you long into their 20s).

This new era of children spending more time alone has been ushered in with a strong emphasis on safety and good habits. For example, when I was growing up, my friends and I would ride two or three on a bicycle, or as many as we could fit, and we had never heard of bike helmets. Today kids (and adults) ride with a helmet and with padding. They understand the benefits of a good diet and exercise, of good fat versus bad fat. They drink bottled water or water from a pitcher that purifies the water. We drank from the garden hose on a hot summer day or from the tap in our kitchen sink (for the younger crowd, the tap is the spout in the sink where the water comes out). Now that caring for our environment has become a bigger issue, our society has moved away from buying bottled water that ultimately will glut our landfills to buying aluminum re-fillable bottles we keep in our home. We fill these bottles with water from our water purification pitcher, bring them with us wherever we go, and then bring them home to start the process the next day (we have about twenty-six of these bottles in my home because the women I live with constantly lose or misplace them, buy new bottles, then find the lost ones). As Hannibal Lecter would tell you, these women I live with love their petty torments.

Some things never change—the grades K–12 experience being one of them. Memories can be made that last a lifetime, but the memories are not always pleasant ones. I think back fondly of having gone to school in the 1970s and 1980s. I vividly remember playing ball during recess and after school (for the younger readers, we actually were able to play a game without necessarily having to wear expensive uniforms or to have our mom drive us to perfectly manicured fields where parents of an eleven-year-old are ready to tell you how great their little Johnny will fit snugly into the New York Yankees lineup in a few years). We had great games (not to mention arguments and fights) in backyards, on school grounds, behind the law firm next to Taco Bell, and even in the street. My dad, being a Bronx boy, always thought of the Long Island kids as unable to survive in the mean streets of his beloved childhood neighborhood, but we had some fun and intense games (and some crazy kids who scared the hell out of me, which helped sweeten the game).

I can also remember all of our school recitals and no-talent shows. What a fun night. Never had so many people with so little talent congregated in one place (I am not counting sessions of Congress). There was always a skinny kid torturing a violin and a fat kid banging on a piano. A courageous boy and girl would sing a duet, sounding like Alfalfa and Darla Hood (*Little Rascals* reference—even my generation didn't get it). But the parents ate it up and took photos at every recital, school play, spelling bee, and ball game.

Today's parents take photos of these special moments as well, but they take them with their phone or tablet for instant review. Those photos are then immediately sent via e-mail to every resident within a twenty-five-mile radius and then posted on Facebook just in case you were not on the e-mail list. My mom and dad had to wait a few weeks for their Kodak moments to develop, then picked them up at the local pharmacy and passed them around the Christmas table, trying to recall when the picture was taken.

I also think back not so fondly on some of the cruel things that were done to me and that I witnessed during my adolescent years. Kids can be cruel and mean no matter what generation you are talking about. I mentioned earlier that kids today are a little more ahead of the game than the kids of my era. They seem a little more confident, make friends easier, and are less intimidated by strangers. Overall they seem to be far ahead of where I was at their age, across the board. They are exposed to things at a much younger age (which is not always a good thing) and are less naïve and innocent (again, not always a good thing). They are more advanced in the area of athletics than we were. In contrast to the no-talent shows that we put on, I have seen school plays, concerts, and dance recitals that my children, niece, and nephews have been in that are full of talented and creative kids. The natural evolution and changing methods of parenting have made today's child much more savvy and almost adult-like.

Unfortunately, this enlightenment has not ended the bullying that some children still must endure, often on a daily basis. The quicker maturation of today's child has not translated into the ceasing, or even the softening, of the desire to ridicule or assault someone who is different, whatever the definition of different is. Bullying is not a new phenomenon. However, like many things today, it has been ramped up and because of technology and other influences, and seems to be at an all-time high. While we have definitely made strides in some areas of acceptance and tolerance, those who are targeted feel the wrath of their classmates like never before. Social media has enabled kids to post unspeakable and depraved thoughts for the world to see. Technology has added the term *cyberbullying* to our lexicon, wherein the abuse is not confined to the school or the schoolyard but now extends into our homes and into the viral world for all to read. We read stories in the newspaper that a young girl or a young boy succumbed to the constant and relentless pressure and took their own life. There can be no justification for this level of intolerance and cruelty. It has been extant for much too long, and our enlightened society should see that it becomes extinct.

CHAPTER 2

THE END OF THE OLD NEIGHBORHOOD

THE OLD NEIGHBORHOOD, and the neighborhood in general, has lost its soul in our ever changing and growing society. I don't necessarily mean the true and traditional Old Neighborhood that my dad and his contemporaries born circa 1940 romanticize about. This is the place where children of immigrants grew up in the Bronx, Brooklyn, the Lower East Side, and on a-hunt-twenty-fifth street. From what I recollect from countless and endless stories, Italians lived on one block, Irish on the next block, Jewish people on the block after that, and so on and so forth. Four- and five-story tenement apartments rose up from the concrete as far as the eye could see. Your entire universe was within a three- or four-block radius of your apartment building. The landscape was dominated by the neighborhood store and the small business owner. There was no Super Stop & Shop, Target, Walmart, or Starbucks to interfere with their existence. Fish was purchased from a fish market, fruit from a fruit stand, and meat from Old Man Bertucci at the butcher shop, who, if you didn't watch closely enough, was not above putting his fat thumb on the scale when he weighed your chopped meat.

Everybody you knew either had a nickname or was identified by their ethnic group. Each neighborhood had an Irish cop, an Italian fish man, and a Jewish gentleman who ran the corner store. My dad had an Uncle Ralph, but they called him Uncle Kenny (or he was Uncle Kenny and they called him Uncle Ralph—I can never keep that straight). He also had an Uncle Tootsie and has a sister named Florence who they called Sass (you just have to accept this on its face as you cannot reason with these old Italians). The thought of locking a door was foreign to the inhabitants of these neighborhoods, as was the thought that the five-and-dime stores—the Woolworth's and the McCrory's—would not only someday be obsolete but be replaced by a huge national chain where you can buy fruit, meat, fish, tires, razor blades, clothes, toothpaste, and bath towels all from the same store. (My Aunt Peggy just rolled over in her grave. By the way, they called her Aunt Lucia.)

According to the tales I heard as a young lad (and I still hear this same stuff to this day), the days were filled with stickball, running through fire hydrants, and all-around good clean American fun. The kids hung out on stoops (for the younger crowd, the stoop is the set of stairs that leads to the front door of the apartment building); the dads and older guys played cards well into the night; and the women cooked, cleaned, sewed, and kept the house (not a great deal for the women—no wonder that men long for these days). Students attended Catholic schools where priests and nuns disciplined with a ruler shot across the knuckles or a slap to the back of the head. Beyond learning the basic subjects, students learned that sexual thoughts should be put out of your mind and that if you read National Geographic you would go blind. The music of the day was dominated by Elvis Presley, Little Richard, Jerry Lee Lewis, and Dion and the Belmonts; their songs served as a backdrop to the long summer nights and were an anthem for the entire 1950s generation.

As people have a habit of romanticizing their childhood, I must take some of these stories and memories with a grain of salt. I never lived in this type of environment, so I only know what I heard, read, or saw in movies or on television regarding this time period. I get the sense that the love and fondness for this era gone by is very genuine, but maybe some of the details have been altered to reinforce the idea that this was the golden age of America. Whether it was or was not can be discussed and debated. There was definitely an innocence and a naiveté that existed, sometimes for the better and sometimes for the worse.

To my dad and his contemporaries, these were the Good Old Days. This was Tom Brokaw's Greatest Generation, the children of post–World War I, World War II, and Korea. There is no doubt about it. If you ask any of them, they would all tell you that the arrow has been pointing down since the dissolution of their beloved old neighborhood. This era represents a slice of Americana that existed in these urban environments that lost some of its energy and luster as the children of this generation moved from the city to the suburbs. Patriotism and trust in our leaders was as high as it ever was before, or will ever be again. This is prior to the 1960s cultural, racial, and sexual revolutions that came sweeping in and changed our society (it knocked our society on its ass). Our country needed these changes, and we needed to look at things more clearly to see if there were improvements that had to be made so that all spheres of our society could fulfill their desire for the American Dream. But the 1960s represented deep-seated change, instability, and unpredictability, whereas the 1950s represented consistency, stability, and predictability.

As the late 1960s and early 1970s approached, the individuals who grew up in the 1950s were getting married and having children. They then began to migrate to the open space of the suburbs. The idea of the urban neighborhood was replaced by the suburban community. These thirtysomethings had graduated from the tenement apartments on Delancey Street and Hell's Kitchen to colonial houses on Oak Tree Lane and Briarwood Drive, complete with backyards and circular driveways. The children of the Greatest Generation still played ball and hung out with friends, but they also swam in pools, joined Little League or the Boy Scouts, and attended sleepovers. The Catholic school experience was replaced with the public school experience. Rulers and head slapping were replaced by yelling and stern talks with the boys' vice principal. The disco tunes which defined the 1970s gave way to the music of Michael Jackson, Madonna, and Phil Collins. Doo-wop gave way to the British Invasion which gave way to disco and now we became the MTV generation, and music videos were played 24 hours per day.

When the children of the 1970s and 1980s grew up and had their own families to raise, most stayed in the suburban world. Our new parenting outlook has created a situation where the teachers are afraid to discipline even the most unruly students. Parents have the "not my kid syndrome" and will be at the school in five minutes if the teacher admonishes their child for not doing their homework or if the teacher has not arrived at the conclusion that their child is the most special, talented, intelligent, gifted, and cute kid who ever graced an elementary school. I would love to comment on the contemporary music that fills the airwaves, iPhones and iPods, but I am not sure of the names of the artists or the songs. My boss likes Lady Gaga, and my wife likes Adele, so there's two.

My neighborhood looks much like the neighborhood I grew up in. Advancement has made the homes a little larger and the cars and SUVs somewhat nicer, but we are more like my dad's generation than his generation was like his dad's generation. The neigh-

borhood and community have undergone more changes. Working longer hours for shorter pay has led to an
interesting dynamic. Since my wife and I work such
long days, with the exception of our next-door-neigh-
bor and one family across the street, we don't know
the name of any of our neighbors. I am embarrassed
to admit this, but it is true. I am not allowed to participate in our neighborhood watch program because I
would constantly be blowing my whistle or calling the
cops because I simply cannot distinguish my neighbors from burglars (some may be both).

My mom grew up in the Bronx. She knew not only
each tenant in her own building but in the next building as well. She knew their relatives, pets, and med-
ical histories. My dad, also a Bronx alum, knew the
store owners on a first name basis, and if he screwed
around, they would be sure to inform his parents or
his priest. Even when I was a kid, we all knew the
names of the families that lived on our block. We
knew what their dad did for a living and what time he
came home for dinner. As we played our forty-eighth
inning of a Wiffle Ball game (for the younger crowd,
the bat is yellow and the ball is white with holes in it
to promote ball movement), we would all wait for the
dinner bell to ring from each home (the dinner bell
was the mom who would open the screen door and
announce that dinner was on the table).

We were always outside playing some kind of sport
or devising ramps and obstacle courses for our bicycles
(just so the under twenty-one gang is not confused, I
am talking about actually being outside participat-

ing in an event, not a Wii or other computer games where you sit on your couch and pretend that you are hitting a home run). In fairness to my children's generation, we didn't have much else to distract us. Our childhood was devoid of cell phones, computers, and tablets, and the only video game we played was Atari, which was so primeval that it cannot be described to today's youth, and any comparison would be silly. The sophistication and real feel of graphics used on video games today blows my mind. But we had to make do with whatever resources were at our disposal, and those resources were usually athletic apparatus and a backyard or open field to play on.

Most of us had a healthy respect for parents and authority in general (I would call it a fear). I chose the word respect because I know how the modern parent winces at the idea that a child could actually have a healthy fear of his parents. Obviously, I am not talking about beating a child, which is unacceptable. Physical and emotional intimidation is not the answer. Yet, the pendulum has swung too far in the other direction. Too many children have little or no respect for their parents, which leads to some of the poor behavior that can be witnessed if you have ever had the good fortune to be at the mall, at the movies, or at a restaurant with a group of teenagers. We have become soft and permissive in assessing behavior. Why have our standards been lowered so much, and when did the children start running the house? A child should not genuinely fear a parent, but a parent should not genuinely fear their child.

CHAPTER 3

SELF-DISCOVERY

SELF-DISCOVERY SEEMS TO be a term that is self-explanatory, but it has different meanings to different people. I have spent a lot of time trying to get to know myself, reflecting on what makes me tick and what is my essence and nature. This has helped me in some tough decision making and crisis management. It seems to me that we would be able to interact with the other members of society in a more fruitful and beneficial way if we had a strong core value system and knowledge of ourselves in a fundamental way. Many poor decisions have their origin in a lack of understanding of what our goals are, what our views truly are, and what type of human being we desire to be or are striving to become. We must know what kind of life we wish to lead and set a plan for achievement. Once our foundation is created, we can gain the confidence and fortitude to dream and the wherewithal to shine. We can become the kind of person who inspires, motivates, and enlightens others and makes them feel they are capable of living an extraordinary life as well (I have just described my wife).

I said that self-discovery may mean something different to different people. A textbook or dictionary would tell you that self-discovery is the act or process of achieving understanding or knowledge of oneself. Sounds great when you answer question # 1 on your Philosophy or Existential Modes of Reality midterm, but what does it really mean at a bare bones rudimentary level? I see it as a vehicle to create self-awareness and to self-reflect (I am overdosing on words beginning with "self").

I believe that a life is rich and rewarding when it is lived with a sense of purpose and a desire for achievement, excellence, consistency, and sexuality (I just wanted to see if you were still paying attention). Some refer to their life's work as a calling. People whose life work provides fulfillment are blessed more than they know. Unfortunately, many of us are just counting off the days at work and just going through the motions. To avoid falling into this insidious trap, we need to have a keen focus and a strong direction. One of the key elements of your journey into self discovery should be to formulate your own well thought out and considered views, mores, and values without the fear of others who may aspire to influence you into their thought process. This exercise is not a luxury; it is a necessity which requires honesty, confidence, and courage.

Going along with the crowd, is easy; blazing your own trail takes chutzpah. It begins with getting to know yourself on every level possible. Lao-Tzu wrote in Tao Te Ching, "He who knows others is learned; he who knows himself is wise." Buddha said, "Your work is to discover your world and then with all your heart give yourself to it." This is some powerful stuff, so I will lighten things a bit with a quote from Lucille Ball (for the tablet generation, she was the star of the *I Love Lucy* program from the 1950s—oh just take my word for it that she is a pioneer) who said "It's a helluva start, being able to recognize what makes you happy."

Despite all our attempts at self-discovery through books, lectures, daytime talk television and prescription meds (and non-prescription meds), we don't devote enough real and meaningful time to this crucial process. Don't get me wrong, most of us are as self-absorbed (another "self" word) and egocentric as possible.

But as much as we are considered a me first generation, we are still lacking in knowing ourselves as well as we could. There is pressure from our early years to conform and to people-please. We begin by attempting to please our parents, siblings, and relatives; and then we move on to pleasing teachers, friends, roommates, co-workers, bosses, subordinates, wives, kids, etc. This is not necessarily a bad thing; and as our society gets a little coarser and more vulgar, more politeness, courtesy, and friendliness go a long way toward creating more positive experiences. However, this should not be done at the expense of personal growth and enrichment, and it should not strip us of our individuality or alter our moral compass.

I am fascinated by the stories behind successful people. My mouth waters when I see their net worth, but their rise to their position fascinates me, particularly if they have an independent or pioneer spirit. I am fascinated by Bill Gates, Steve Jobs, Phil Knight, and Sam Walton. But I also can immerse myself in the words of Tony Robbins, Joel Osteen, Deepak Chopra, and Wayne Dyer. These individuals, in one form or another, followed their dreams with a strong purpose and without fear of reprisals. Their words convey a sense of fulfillment about the path they are on and the journey they are undertaking. They have passion, enthusiasm, intelligence, and creativity; and they emit a positive life force. Listening to their words you can get a sense of how they reached the peak of their field or discipline. There is a fearlessness about them, an understanding that to live a meaningful and extraordinary life, they would have to deal with risks and with others who might discourage them from following their dreams. They convey a confidence and a belief in themselves that has its roots in self-awareness and self-discovery Like my wife, they have drive, ambition and perseverance. I would surmise that at an early age they began to formulate a vision of the kind of life they wanted to live and the type of person they wanted to be.

These individuals and others of their ilk are a source of inspiration for me, because I tend to be an over-analyzer (to put it mildly) and a conservative person. Risk takers intrigue me because they stay true to their vision without fear or with the ability to manage their fear so that it does not interfere with their higher purpose. Also, they know what they want and go for it. Sounds trite, but most of us (myself included) have the ability to talk ourselves out of taking risks. Successful people find a solution to a problem and find reasons why problems can be dealt with, while others obsess over the problem and find reasons why problems cannot be dealt with. For many of us, even if we know what we want, we don't know how to develop a plan to get it, or we eschew the necessary sacrifices it would take to achieve our dreams. Sadly, most people don't ever take the time to reflect on their life and know what they want out of life, and I mean really want, deep down in the abyss of your soul. Mark Twain said, "I can teach anybody how to get what they want out of life. The problem is that I can't find anybody who can tell me what they want."

Obviously, there is no absolute plan or formula for personal or professional success. In addition, there is no precise definition for personal or professional success. In my view and in my experience, self-knowledge would provide a strong foundation for happiness. We probably can agree that there are many unhappy people who may not know why they are unhappy, may know why they are unhappy but cannot construct a plan to get out of their situation, or, worse yet, have long given up any attempts to improve their plight.

As I have gotten older (I mean more sophisticated), I have spent many hours thinking about things such as what brings me joy, what saddens me, what kind of husband and father I want to be, my career choice, my dreams and whether are they still attainable, and where I see myself down the road. I wish I had done this at a much younger age, and I am eternally grateful that I was fortunate enough to marry the best woman in the world and have the best daughters in the world (sometimes a little luck is the best plan). But my lack of self-discovery and my reluctance (fear) of pursuing my dreams led me to very poor choices, both in my personal and professional life. I am sure we all have experienced this phenomenon—dead-end jobs and dead-end relationships, both of which are easy to get into but impossible to be extricated from without paying an emotional toll. We then carry this jaded feeling and emotional baggage with us through life, and oftentimes we can crumble from the weight of the disappointment.

To understand yourself and to be comfortable in your own skin breeds confidence and self-esteem, wonderful and powerful tools that facilitate healthier relationships, both personal and professional, and good, well thought out decision making. It would help us to avoid falling into common traps: bad relationships and worse jobs.

I read an article that said many people, after death and public speaking, fear being by themselves the most. I don't mean to grow old alone or die alone, because nobody wants that fate. I mean that they constantly must be in contact with another human being. As someone who loves the serenity and tranquility of a long walk, I found this very odd. But when I gave it more thought, it made sense. Think of all the people who spend their lives talking on their cell phone, texting, or staring down at their phone or tablet for an extended period of time. I don't mean just young people. Most people in my age range can't stand to be alone with their thoughts for five seconds. I guess they are afraid that they may get an original thought and have to actually improve themselves.

I can easily amuse myself. Fear of being alone without a twenty-four-hour-a-day connection to the world is born out of fear and a lack of confidence, which is a perfect recipe for poor decision making. Many fear being alone to such a degree that they stay in unhealthy relationships, figuring it is a better alternative than being alone. Sometimes you have to take a step back to take two steps forward. Between relationships, we should be assessing what went wrong and caused the demise of the relationship, and working to build a new relationship with someone who possesses characteristics and values that match our own. Often we jump right into another dating situation without truly taking the time to decide the type of person we wish to spend time with and without taking the time to decide what type of person and partner we wish to be.

Years of bad break-ups and bitter disappointments kill our confidence and self-esteem. Take the time to revive your faith and belief in yourself and to get to like yourself again (Sally Field understands this). Once you accomplish this, you have a better shot at a healthy or productive relationship (although most of the women I know have given up on men completely).

We should operate with the same thought process when we evaluate our professional life. The bosses at dead end crappy jobs prey on the weak and hopeless. These jobs exist to take our soul, one piece at a time until we are left with a black hole, devoid of sunlight. We begin to feel insignificant, irrelevant and without value. The employer assumes you have nowhere else to go, no ambition, no drive, no dream to pursue, and no passion for a better existence. In fact, the assumption is that you should be grateful to work very long hours for very short pay. Since he or she has you by the you-know-whats, you are forced to stay put and stand pat. This is a life lived in limbo between existence and subsistence (if you sense anger, you are on target; believe me, I have been there many times). The worker feels he has no real value, is grateful to have a job at all, and is at the mercy of the employer.

This becomes a vicious cycle that can break your will and your spirit. It is hard, in our economic climate, to break this pattern. Opportunities and options give you leverage and bargaining power in life. The best way to get out of this quagmire is to never get into it.

Hopefully, our children's generation and the generations beyond will avoid this dire fate by availing themselves of a very powerful weapon, the human mind. President Kennedy said, "Man is still the most extraordinary computer of all." We should use our extraordinary computer to live an extraordinary life. Self-discover, self-assess, self-reflect, and really think and consider what you want to do with your life. Add your own special verse to life's poem. Get all the education you can (both in school and out of school), and apply yourself. This will start when we have confidence, self-esteem and self-worth. You don't have to accept dead-end jobs and dead-end relationships. Ultimately, you will give yourself an opportunity to do what few are lucky enough to do, which is to enjoy and get true fulfillment and satisfaction from your life's work.

CHAPTER 4

Animals and Pets

I HAVE TRIED TO be honest in sharing my thoughts throughout this book, so I must admit to being one of those annoying people who love animals. I don't mean the type that makes you feel guilty for ordering a steak or who throws blood on you if you wear a fur coat. Rather, I am fascinated by their innate ability to learn, think, communicate, and interact (which is especially impressive since many of our young people go to high priced colleges and private learning institutions and even with the ability to speak are devoid of these talents).

I can watch for hours at the Bronx Zoo while the gorillas eat, rest, and coexist. I have observed them eating in groups of four, two parents and two children (humans don't even do this anymore). My daughter Deborah and I were watching with particular interest on one occasion as one of the gorilla children misbehaved at the dinner table and stole food from his sibling. The Big Papa Silverback arose from his seat, turned junior around, slapped him on the butt for correction, and then proceeded to finish his lunch.

Junior got the point and did the same. It was as if I was glimpsing my childhood, except the gorillas had superior table manners to my family's.

Animal lovers have benefited from the many television channels that take the viewer into the animals' natural habitat. These programs have taught me various facts which I bore people with and repeat like Rain Man every chance I get, such as these: the arms of a gorilla are longer than their legs; gorillas are herbivores; elephants hold onto memories, some for their entire lives; they experience grief and mourning for lost family and friends; a lion's roar can carry four to five miles; and no two tigers have the same stripes— they are like fingerprints to a human. What always strikes me is how human these animals seem. If they could talk they would take over the world. Hopefully, they would be better to us than we have been to them.

There are a lot more programs on television today that deal with animals as their primary subject matter. There seem to be more people interested in animals and who desire to make some aspect of working with animals their life's work. My generation received much of our knowledge and information from *Wild Kingdom*, a show hosted by Marlin Perkins and geared toward the casual animal fan. He wore a nice suit and narrated and educated from a studio, as opposed to the contemporary hosts who teach while in the process of wading knee deep in a river of crocodiles or who grab a cobra by the throat and encourage him to open wide so the audience can get a clear look at his venomous fangs. These folks are really wrapped up in their careers. I saw a man wearing Buffalo Bill infrared night goggles while standing about ten feet away from a lion in the middle of the African plains. He was talking quietly so he would not disturb Simba, especially since Simba is a night predator who would have loved to finish off Mr. Bill and mount him in his den, right next to his Derek Jeter autographed poster. I absolutely love lions—their arrogance, laziness, toughness, and the way the men make the women do the hard work. They are fascinating to look at and observe, but from afar, very afar.

My hat is off to these true animal enthusiasts, who, even after multiple attacks, go right back to their job, even excusing the animal's aggression. I admire anyone who loves their vocation to this degree. The world needs more people with this level of commitment to their work and who have chosen the noble pursuit of helping to ensure that these beautiful animals are not in danger of being needlessly harmed or becoming extinct.

I grew up visiting the Bronx Zoo with my parents and grandparents and have taken my family there on many occasions. I would hate to think that our grandchildren and their children would be robbed of the joy of seeing an elephant, tiger, gorilla, lion, bear, or seal for the first time, and then bringing their children to the same place many years later to experience the same feeling of wonder and amazement.

As much as I enjoy seeing and learning about these more exotic animals, they could never bring me the unconditional love, warmth, friendship, and loyalty that I have been blessed to feel from the three dogs who have graced our home.

The dogs who inhabited Delaware Avenue, my childhood stomping grounds, were traditional pets who ate their meals outside and were more popular when they were seen and not heard, or heard and not seen. They were often left outside for many hours, sometimes in cold or wet weather. When one died, there was no mourning period or period of adjustment. A replacement dog was sought whenever the owner got around to it. There was not much thought given to the naming process, as many seemed to be named Fido, Rusty, or Tiny. Their bathroom and grooming habits were nobody's business but their own, and if they did not have matching leashes and collars, everyone just dealt with it. They did not go on car trips, vacations, play dates, or to a pet store to wander the aisles with their owner. The family dog was a pet in the traditional sense of the word, and treated like an animal (a Hollywood starlet just fainted at this thought as she walks on Rodeo Drive with Little Lulu in her jacket pocket or shares a sip of her Starbucks triple latte cappuccino frappuccino with skim milk).

Today's family dog enjoys a much more lavish lifestyle. They eat special foods that are grain free, chock full of vitamins and minerals. Their diet consists of foods that are high in protein and low in carbohydrates, a kind of canine Atkins or South Beach diet. Their water bowl is filled with water poured from a water purification pitcher or from a bottle. Tap water is on the endangered species list. My wife on occasion will provide our dog, Cashmere, with a lobster bib to avoid any unpleasantness during her evening meal.

The weather is scrupulously monitored to avoid long durations of heat or cold. If it is too hot, we try to walk our dogs on the grass to avoid the hot pavement. If it is too cold, the dogs are equipped with jackets that would make the Kardashians blush. They are never, and I mean never, allowed outside in the rain for more than a few minutes to take care of their necessities.

Death is treated very seriously. My beloved dog Minnie died on June 18, 2006 (on Father's Day of all things). I took the next day off from work and still mourn her and miss her. I used to bring her all over town, so many store owners and residents got to know her. When I told my friend that Minnie has passed away (and this guy is a teamster type, if you know what I mean), he sobbed uncontrollably. He had told me several months earlier about the death of his mother with less tears and emotion. My sister, Sarah, had a wonderful dog named Brodie. When he passed away in 2012, we spoke on the phone for fifteen minutes without either one of us being able to complete a sentence. They are just so easy to love, and they love you unconditionally.

The naming of the family dog has become a family discussion. Every member of the family puts forth a nomination, and then the name is chosen. Our two dogs, Cashmere and Venus, were named by yours truly. But most naming discussions are similar to the discussions held when baby names are being considered. Just as baby names such as John, Thomas, Michael, and Mathew have been replaced by Morgan, Madison, Schuyler, Dakota, Cheyenne, and Noah, dog names have gone from Fido and Tiny to Charlie (my neighbor's German Shepherd), in an effort to truly humanize the dog, and Champ (my sister's new dog) in an effort to tell the dog his rightful destiny.

Our dogs also benefit from private grooming sessions. While Minnie had to endure the shame of being bathed by me in our bathtub, Cashmere and Venus are taken to PetSmart, where they are taken care of by a terrific girl named Alex, who just loves them to death. She continues the spoiling of our dogs that began at home. They run to her when they see her, knowing that not since the Pharaohs has anyone received such special treatment. When I come to pick them up from their grooming and bathing session, they not only look and smell wonderful, but they are wearing bandanas, usually with the design or color of the season or holiday we are closest to. I am provided with a report card that details their day of luxury, including their activities, likes and dislikes, personalities, and overall temperament. Not to be outdone by any other dog owner, I proudly announce my dogs' report cards to the cashier and other patrons. I also mentioned their remarkable progress at Christmas dinner, right between the saying of grace and the eating of the shrimp cocktail. Our dogs also get the benefit of multiple leashes and collars, as well as special collars only to be worn while taking their Christmas photos.

I can count the number of times on one hand that an owner walked their dog when I was growing up in my Long Island neighborhood. The dog either was relegated to the backyard in perpetuity or was just let out of the house with instructions to be home before dinner. We walk our dogs several nights a week and on both weekend days, if possible. We also take our dogs on car trips, play dates, with their friends, to the beach, to the park, and sometimes on vacation with us. They are members of our family in every sense of the word. They are taken to PetSmart or Petco, where they are allowed to browse the aisles and even make an occasional purchase, as long as they have proper identification.

While there is some hyperbole, most of this is absolutely true. Speaking for my family, we love animals and all that they contribute to our home. My older daughter, Deborah, out on her own, now has her own dog, Piper. My younger daughter, Krista, also out on her own and a taskmaster when it comes to training, has a bearded dragon and is in negotiation with her boyfriend, Jamieson, to acquire a pooch.

The reason we go to all this trouble and fuss is not only the love we feel for them but also the love they give us in return, along with their loyalty, friendship, warmth, and understanding. From seeing-eye dogs to service dogs to bomb sniffing dogs to family pets, they are all fascinating to me. They provide a calmness and serenity when the world becomes loud and chaotic. They provide an approval when the world disapproves and a warmth and comfort when society is cold and distant.

Like children, they can all grow up in the same house and all be so different. Minnie, my Labrador Retriever–German Shepherd–St. Bernard mix, was a king among kings. Fearless and brave, even at the end when her bloated stomach literally twisted her intestines inside her, she never whimpered or cried. She was the strong, silent type, a trait more humans should cultivate. We were all there when she peacefully went to her next life, where I am sure that she lives with the dignity and courage with which she lived this one. A better friend I never had.

Conversely, Cashmere, my yellow lab, is neither fearless nor brave and is as stubborn as the day is long. I presented her to my wife ten years ago for her birthday. Truth be told, I had a different dog in mind, but Michelle fell in love at first sight, and as you husbands know, that was that. It turned out to be one of the best decisions she (I mean we) ever made. Now, Cashmere can ignore instructions as well as your own teenagers do. Yet, her capacity to love you and fill you with happiness is unparalleled. She is so gentle, kind, and intelligent. Every time I bring her someplace, she is the center of attention. Like the great horse Secretariat, Cashmere has a sixth sense about seeking attention and being a ham at just the right time. She is really a charmer and loves being fawned over. My sister, my daughter's boyfriend, and Alex, our groomer, have their designs on stealing Cashmere or making an offer for her, which is totally out of the question (especially at the lowball numbers they have offered).

My black lab, Venus, is a rescue dog brought to my doorstep in 2006 by my daughter with a sob story about the dog's lonely, isolated, and checkered past. What could I do? I love my children, and they are terrific kids (when they're not driving me out of my mind, but I digress). So we all decided to keep this runaway and we named her Venus because Venus is the goddess of love in mythology (Greek or Roman, I can never keep it straight), and Venus will just lick you and kiss you to death. She would make Richard Dawson feel inadequate (for you kids, he hosted *Family Feud* about six hosts ago and kissed everyone and everything not nailed down). She follows my wife around, every step of the way, including into the bathroom. Venus will spoon and cuddle with you in bed and is the most affectionate dog I have ever seen. She still suffers some ill effects from her days on the street, but she is overwhelmingly obedient and loving. In full disclosure, she may have nipped my nephew, my mother in law, and my daughter's best friend, but they probably deserved it. They all apologized to Venus for their actions, and we have moved on.

CHAPTER 5

POLITICS, RELIGION,
AND SPIRITUALITY

AT AN EARLY age I was told by my parents not to discuss religion or politics outside of the home because there are many varied beliefs and also because they could be controversial subjects. To this day, I try to adhere to this edict, but people seem to relish conversations on these subjects. I have heard politics and religion discussed freely in the workplace, while I am waiting on line at the movie theater or at the supermarket, and on athletic fields.

While I am neither a religious person nor a particularly political person, I respect the feelings of those who are, and I respect different belief systems. However, I have absolutely no respect or regard for those who espouse a way of life and then are totally hypocritical in how they live their life. Talk is cheap; actions make you what you are.

An individual with different views on religion or political thought than me is fine, as long as he lives a life aligned with the principles he espouses. There is nothing worse than a religious phony. You know the type—all family values, morals, and integrity until his girlfriend, Swiss bank account, and dress and high heels are discovered. These are the type of people that use religion for gain rather than letting religion act their conscience. They bring religion out of the closet every once in a while, like a winter coat.

Even if a person is not a phony and lives in concert with his true beliefs, I wish that the conversations regarding religion and politics could be more civil and tolerant, rather than vitriolic and judgmental. Unfortunately, the latter sort is in evidence much too often. For example, Fox News has their talking heads and MSNBC has their talking heads. I just wish that the talk was more often a healthy and two way dialogue in an effort to facilitate a better society, a better America, and a better humanity. Instead, it is often a forum for a political or religious agenda, grandstanding, and the glorification of their own ideology, often without room for compromise or for an opposing ideology. It is seen as a game, our political party versus yours, our religion versus yours. I think a lot of us feel that this is a game with no winners and with the American people feeling like the losers.

Religious liberty, including the liberty not to believe, is one of the cornerstones of our Constitution and our way of life. Although I am not a religious person, I realize the importance of the freedom of religious expression and the separation of church and state. In the last few years, it seems as if the line between politics and religion has blurred, and the two often seem to invade the world of the other.

Some of the shows I have seen on television and articles I have read politicize religion. For example, as many gay and lesbian teenagers have become the targets of bullying, several enlightened states are attempting to introduce anti-bullying legislation. All we need to do to realize just how important and necessary this legislation is would be to remember the tragic death of Rutgers student Tyler Clementi, an eighteen-year-old student at Rutgers University who jumped to his death on September 22, 2010. Three days earlier, Clementi's roommate and fellow hallmate used a webcam and a computer to view, without Clementi's knowledge, Clementi kissing another man. On September 21, the day prior to his suicide, the roommate urged friends and Twitter followers to watch via webcam a second tryst between Clementi and his friend. Clementi's death has brought national and international attention to the issues of cyberbullying (which affects all children across the board) and in particular the struggles facing gay and lesbian teenagers.

Clementi's parents issued a statement the day of the announcement of the verdict in the trial of Clementi's roommate (I can't even begin to comprehend the depth of their pain; losing a child is the worst thing that can happen to a person). More parents will endure the same pain if we do not heed their words. Joseph Clementi said, "You're going to meet a lot of people in your lifetime. Some of the people you may not like. Just because you do not like them does not mean you have to work against them. When you see somebody doing something wrong, tell them: That's not right. Stop it! The change you want to see in the world begins with you."

Jane Clementi said, "In this digital world, we need to teach our youngsters that their actions have consequences, that their words have real power to hurt or to help. They must be encouraged to choose to build people up and not tear them down."

I admire the courage and the fortitude of the Clementis, and I wish them and others in their situation peace and solace. Hopefully, these wishes are attainable. Teenage bullying is an epidemic, and the death toll is climbing.

Even with this tragic backdrop, I have seen conservative Christian lobbyists and others on television and in the print media who are encouraging their lawmakers to thwart any anti-bullying legislation. Their rationale is that this type of legislation either encourages or does not properly discourage a gay lifestyle.

Wait a minute here, folks. I thought we were all God's children. I thought that we were all made in God's image. If I recall my early religious training, the idea of religion is to promote good will and foster love, understanding, peace, and harmony. I did not realize that certain groups were not entitled to those lofty ideals. Frankly, it is my opinion that this anti-gay feeling is actually hate wrapped up in some phony notion of religious belief or morality.

We can all decide who we want to spend time with and the type of life we wish to pursue, and we are perfectly within our rights to have a negative feeling about a particular lifestyle or set of values (even if oftentimes we are close-minded and intolerant towards views not our own). However, we have absolutely no right to intimidate, threaten, coerce, or force someone to live a life they are not meant to live.

As an example, consider the opponents to gay marriage. The right wing is always talking about the Constitution and that our freedom is being eroded. They espouse the notion that we should be able to live professionally and personally without over-regulation by the government and without strong restrictions from the government. I could not agree more. But doesn't the right to choose the individual that we wish to spend the rest of our life with fall under our cherished First Amendment freedoms? Nothing could be more freely expressed than the expression of love one has for the person they want to grow old with. This idea should be right up the alley of the right wing. The Constitution grants us this freedom; therefore, the government (Big Brother) should not infringe on the precious right of two consenting adults to wed and merge every aspect of their lives. But hold on one second, Louis Bruno, I was once told by a co-worker. He explained that his religion, not his politics, guided his anti–gay marriage stance. I guess when you want to deny someone their civil rights, just camouflage your ignorance, intolerance, and hate with religion. The left wing should run to support gay marriage, but they don't have the chutzpah. As times have changed and the public perception of gay marriage has changed slightly, some of the politicians on both sides have softened their stance on opposing gay marriage (I know that you are all surprised that a politician would bow to the whims of polls). I have come to the conclusion that it is inevitable that the political sphere and the religious sphere will always interact. I just hope that reason, flexibility, and tolerance will eventually trump the rigid, inflexible and intolerant tenor of contemporary political and religious discourse. A dogma that is inclusionary rather than exclusionary will yield our best opportunity for the moderates who wish to intelligently debate and discuss issues to squeeze out the extremists from all political parties and religious groups whose lack of interest in and understanding of true freedom and liberty is exceeded by their desire to demonize those who oppose their viewpoint.

I have great respect for those who live their life with true reverence for their religious or political beliefs but still are capable of respecting opposing religious or political views. To these folks, religion is a great source of comfort and serenity and provides strength when they are faced with conflict, crisis, or tragedy.

My mom is like this. Raised as a good Catholic girl in the Bronx, she has been a model Catholic for over seventy years (I get no more lasagna if I reveal her exact age). Her religion and faith are important to her, but she never makes the assumption that your religion and faith are less important than hers. She also eschews making moral judgments and labeling people, which have become two of our favorite national pastimes. She also has the ability to evolve and change her mind about an issue that years ago she may have felt differently about.

The ability to change with the times and see things from a different perspective is very important. Free thinking and critical thinking are strong weapons in making decisions and living a more fruitful and less closed off life. One of my early religious teachers used to tell us that religion is an important way to learn to love. It is a vehicle toward a world where we could become connected to others in a special way. What a great message to impart to young people, the thought that we could use religion to make the world a better place to live. I am sure that this message still is taught today; unfortunately many just don't hear it.

Contrary to popular belief, spirituality and religion can peacefully co-exist. Many of the ideas and tenets are similar; it is just the terminology that differs. A lot of people today who were raised in a traditional religious setting have either chosen to live a spiritual life or have incorporated some spiritual values with their religious values (which is very understandable since many of the fundamental beliefs translate). If I were to tell someone that I do not follow a specific religion but rather that I am on a spiritual path, I get the same look that a teacher once gave me when I showed up to fifth grade wearing a pair of chaps. This is understandable since a lot of spirituality has its roots in the religions of the Eastern world, such as Buddhism, and is not a major part of the religions of the western world.

We get set in our ways and in things we have known for a long time, and we are often intimidated by new ideas, are quick to dismiss them as strange or view them as a rejection of what we have been taught throughout our lives.

When my wife lost her twenty-two-year-old brother, Walter, in 1999, she turned to spirituality to help in the healing process. Her wounds were deep. She had been raised in a Protestant environment and had sent our daughters to Sunday School, which they got a lot out of. But in this instance, along with the love and support of her family and friends and the guidance of her lifelong religious practices, she would need and require additional support from a new source. My wife found comfort in the teachings and practices of spirituality and continues to find the same serenity in it today.

I have joined my wife and children on their spiritual path for quite a few years. I see spirituality as a journey of self-discovery, a tool in balancing your personal and professional life and your mind and body and a means to connect to both yourself and others. It has aided me greatly in my effort to put meaning into my life and to provide me with a sense of direction and purpose. Like many others, I struggled for many years in trying to find a sense of order in the disorder of life, and while life is a constant process of trial and error (and in my case a lot of error), at least I have some ammunition to fight the tide that can sometimes overwhelm us.

Spirituality has helped me see the good in others and to see how much we need each other. Being cynical and negative is very easy in our culture, and we have many occasions and opportunities to display these feelings. However, as we travel down our spiritual path, we begin to value the notion that we are on a mission to make the world and our earth a better place to call home, to make a world that rewards compassion and values and respects all life.

The genesis in attempting to reach this goal is to have a vision of the kind of world that we want to live in, the type of world that we want our children and grandchildren to inherit.

We must first have a sense of self and shift our thinking from the obsession with the individual to the passion of making ourselves better people in an effort to effect change on a grass roots level that ultimately will lead to change on a more massive scale. We are all connected on a certain level, and we are interdependent. Living a life of service to mankind is the highest form of living, the highest success that you can achieve. Sharing, helping, and serving not only benefit your fellow humans on an altruistic level but they also benefit you on a selfish level. You will feel terrific and have a sense of fulfillment, especially with the knowledge that you have made a connection with someone, who may pay the good deed forward, creating a chain reaction of good will.

I try to have a positive inner core and to create positive energy. We can achieve great things if we approach life with passion, enthusiasm, energy, reason, and compassion and apply and direct these attributes both inward to help ourselves in our journey and outward to help others in their journey.

There is plenty of space in the world for religion and spirituality to coexist and at times overlap. I get a special feeling from my spiritual experience and existence, a feeling I did not get from the Catholic teachings I learned as a young boy. Many have a special place in their heart for their religious principles, and that is just fine. Either way, the goal of creating a special world for us all to exist and flourish within, where we help our fellow citizens and seek to create rather than to destroy is a universal dream. The name we give this quest may differ and the methods we choose to fulfill our dream and purpose may differ, but we must all be galvanized and unrelenting in our desire for a better tomorrow and our hope for a better world for future generations. We all share the same world. I say we make it one we can be proud of.

CHAPTER 6

HORRIBLE FORMER JOBS

THERE IS A wonderful line in the classic Woody Allen movie *Annie Hall*. His character (Alvy Singer) says to Diane Keaton's character (Annie Hall) that life is divided up into the horrible and the miserable. Unfortunately, these adjectives describe almost every job I have had as far back as I can remember (present employer excepted, of course). It began in my teens and early twenties with fast food restaurants, supermarkets, and drug stores and continued following my college graduation with jobs—prison sentences—in banking and elsewhere, including several other jobs that I have blocked out with the help of mental health professionals.

I understand that when you are a teenager there will be some jobs you will do that aren't much fun, and that is fine. It builds character and work ethic and teaches the value of a dollar. Once kids start to have to pay for some of their own clothes, sneakers, etc., they will go from saying, "Daddy, these sneakers are only $100, to "Daddy, can you believe these sneakers are $100"?

However, once we start on our career path, there should be a sense of purpose and fulfillment. While no career or job is perfect, since we are going to be going to a place every day for about forty years, the least we could ask for is to get *something* out of the experience. I am not asking for *Willy Wonka and the Chocolate Factory*, but getting up every morning dreading the upcoming day is an unhealthy way to live.

Fortunately, for the last several years, I have worked at a nice place with friendly people doing a job I enjoy (for the most part). Don't get me wrong, it's not the starting shortstop for the Yankees or a great movie role, but there is a sense of accomplishment at the end of the day (what do you want from me, I need this job. If you really want to help me, tell your friends and family to buy this book and I will tell you what I really think of my job). All kidding aside, it's not a bad place to go each day. But I can't say that about a lot of my former jobs.

For many years, I worked for a large American bank (actually three banks, as there were two mergers during my tenure). While I hated every minute of my approximately eight years at Alcatraz, part of it was my fault, because banking is not in my blood. But I did not have the courage to pursue my dreams or stand up to those pushing me into banking. I was just out of college, and I needed a job. As the old saying does, "Be careful what you wish for because you might get it." Well, I got it, you know where. A first job out of college is always a reality check, like getting cold water thrown in your face; but I knew there had to be a better existence than hoping that I would get into an auto accident on the way to work to avoid showing up (even then I would have had to make up the time).

I respect people who make their living doing customer service on the phone, because that's where I started. And I did not excel. Going from senior year of college to this real world experience was a bit overwhelming. I could not believe the things people would say to me: cursing, yelling, screaming, and ethnic epithets (and that was just the women). Wearing a headset and being chained (literally) to my desk sucked.

What an awful way to make a living. It is an honest living and a valuable job, but it just was not for me. It did not fit my personality. That is why I implore my children and anyone who will listen to have the courage of their convictions and chase their dream. Go after it with everything you have. It may not work out, but you will never know if you don't pursue it.

Not only did we make slightly more money than prisoners, but the expectations were disproportionate to the money we earned and the way we were treated. We were expected to handle a certain number of calls per hour, yet if some yahoo wanted to spend a half hour on the phone discussing his Persian rug or why his son is a big disappointment, we had to indulge them (within reason).

In addition, many of our calls were recorded or monitored, supposedly to ensure quality but in reality to give the bosses more fodder to correct (abuse) the customer service reps. They would play back our calls to us, going over each word said to the customer as if peace in the Middle East rested on the outcome. Each syllable was dissected in an effort to ensure that you had absolutely no idea what to tell the customer regarding his inquiries. Correct information was not enough. They wanted to hear your smile, they wanted a nice lilt in your voice, they wanted you to tell a customer his correct balance with style and panache. An exceedingly high expectation for about $17,000 per year.

I would like to share a completely true story about what a farce this entire system was. In one of my interactions with a customer, he asked for something, and I responded, "No problem." As luck would have it, this was one of the calls being taped by one of my bosses. She played back the call for me, told me that she had a problem with me saying, "no problem" to the customer, and failed this call. I did not understand, since the customer got his correct information, I was sure that I had a nice smile and special lilt in my voice, and we ended on a positive note. But still I failed this call. My attempts to overturn this failed call were rebuffed. While I was not forced to wear the scarlet letter *F*, I was still miffed. But I moved on, chalking up the experience to an overzealous boss who in her desire for grandeur had trampled on Louis S. Bruno (that's me).

Less than one month later, this same bank that employed me had a commercial wherein my customer service department was featured. An individual who had a problem and an inquiry called a customer service rep for assistance. After the customer detailed what his issues were and what help he needed, the customer service rep responded, "No problem."

Wait a minute, I said to myself. These very same words that were uttered by yours truly only one month ago which had resulted in a failed call and had cost me a chance at a food processor were now being used in a commercial to highlight the good work being done in my department. How could this be? Had my boss and her superiors gone completely mad? Had they not seen the script for this well directed commercial? Well, I was not going to take this lightly, so on Monday morning I had every intention of speaking with Cruella De Ville and asking her to reconsider her stance in light of the fact that someone in our marketing department shared my view that "no problem" is an acceptable response to a customer. However, to my chagrin, I had a new boss on Monday morning, my old boss had been promoted to a different unit, and the tape of my failed call had gone the way of the Nixon tapes.

Well, we live and learn, but this and other experiences took their toll on me. It was not just the failing of the call, as we all make mistakes. I am fine with that. It was the attitude that I got from my boss and her boss. They loved the idea that they had the power to hurt the customer service reps, to make us feel unimportant and insignificant. They threw compliments around like manhole covers, but reveled in ridiculing good workers, especially new ones who had a deer in the headlights look at first. The units and departments were run by small-minded people with even smaller ideas and an even smaller sense of humanity. Their knowledge of banking and their job was weak, and their leadership and communication skills were even worse. I would love to rid the world of these types, but they exist in all walks of life. It is our job to banish them to a place where they can only hurt each other. Good riddance.

Since we were attached to the computer and our desk with our headset, we had to sign into our workspace with a code. Each time you left your desk you would sign out, and then you would sign back in when you returned to your desk. Every day you would get a printout of the previous day's sign-ins and sign-outs, including your lunch, which was forty-five minutes, including the time it took to get past the guards and swim across the moat. One of my supervisors would circle a part of the printout that she wanted an explanation for with a red pen (like a fourth grade teacher). For example, one day I took forty-six minutes for lunch. I had signed out at 1:06 but had not signed back in until 1:52. A red circle around the two times appeared on my printout the next day with the words "Where were you" printed underneath them with three question marks. Did this idiot mean where was I for the one extra minute? For sixty seconds? How does one answer such a question?

When queried, I explained to my supervisor that I did not recall where I had spent that precious forty-sixth minute of my lunch break, but I assured him that it would never happen again. Since he was very magnanimous, he let me off with a warning because of my good standing at the bank, but he did reinforce the idea that this lollygagging would not be tolerated on his watch. I expressed my appreciation for his dispensation and went on with my day. Can you imagine this stupidity? To earn seventeen grand a year and put up with this nonsense. Meanwhile, the management team spent its time in "executive" and "emergency" meetings (poker games) and taking four-star lunches on the company dime. You wonder why people get demoralized and disillusioned.

Several years after I was sprung from the general customer service unit, I moved onto (was banished to) a more specialized customer service unit. My cubicle was next to the cubicle of a vice president, who was a very nice and friendly woman but did not know a checkbook from a pot roast. Yet she had risen to VP. Many joked that she kept getting promoted to keep her away from customers, where her lack of banking knowledge could do some real damage. She took a two-week vacation in August one year, and on the last day of the vacation (the tenth business day that she had not been in the office), her boss came to look for her. I explained to this gentleman that she was on vacation. Since it was Friday and after 4:oo p.m., Mr. Boss Man assumed that she had left early for her vacation, which would begin the following Monday. I guess he didn't exactly have his finger on the pulse of his employees, since the VP in question had been away for ten days and was returning to the office the following Monday.

Just think about this scenario. The VP misses ten days of work and nobody knows or notices. She must be doing some very serious and important work. Just a tip for you young kids going into the workforce. If your boss does not notice that you have been gone for two weeks, it is safe to assume that you are not one of the main cogs in the machine. The most important lesson is that it is socially acceptable for a VP to miss ten business days without any impact being felt, yet the lowest paramecium on the hierarchy must not abuse the system by taking an unauthorized extra sixty seconds during lunch. To avoid future problems, I wore diapers to work so that I would not take advantage of my customer service position and spend any extra time in the bathroom.

When I finally was paroled from customer service to a more administrative position in the next building, I found it to be just another cellblock. Since the work did not interest me, nor did I understand a lot of it, the chance for this being a good experience was poor. However, I found the people to be a little easier to deal with and the rules far more flexible. The atmosphere was more human, and we were treated like adults (which didn't seem like an unreasonable request). Yet some of the bullshit still existed, only in a different form. Through a co-worker I had befriended, I met an employee from another department who shared a very funny story with me. He told me with a smile on his face, "Lou, wait until you hear this one." This individual worked in an area where many problems arose, and his mandate was to eradicate these problems and see that they did not recur.

Here is the story he told me: One day he went to his boss and told him that they had a problem. His boss responded by saying that from now on there would not be "problems" but rather "situations." It had a better ring to it and the connotation was not so negative. About a month later, my friend went to his boss and told him that they had a situation. His boss responded by saying that from now on there would not be "situations" but rather "obstacles." People overcome obstacles and that is just what their department was created for. Sounds good. About a month later, my friend went to his boss and told him that he had an obstacle. His boss responded by saying that from now on there would not be "obstacles" but rather "challenges." People were born to accept and conquer any challenge, and that is just what their department was created for. About a month later, my friend went to his boss and told him that they had a challenge. His boss responded by saying that from now on there would not be "challenges" but rather *opportunities to excel.* This crap is so brilliant that whoever thought of it should have a statue in front of the waterfall in the lobby of the building. I asked my friend if next month he would go to his boss and tell him that they have an opportunity to excel. He reminded me that he had over thirty-five years of service with the bank, so instead of going to his boss with news of an opportunity to excel, he went to his boss with news of his retirement.

Every Wednesday morning we would have a meeting. If an issue or problem (I mean an opportunity to excel) arose, the individual who ran the meeting would advise that the matter was now being addressed by a focus group. Wow, I thought, finally we were going to get some action. However, the next week I was invited to sit in on the focus group meeting, where it was agreed that the matter being discussed was more complex than first thought and would need to be addressed by a task force. A task force—now we are getting somewhere. As you might expect, the next week's task force meeting did not yield any results, so the gentleman in charge of this roundtable discussion decided that due to the delicate nature of this matter, a steering committee needed to be formed to dissect all areas of this issue. Much to my dismay, I never found out the results of the steering committee's investigation, but something tells me that a firm and concrete decision about how to tackle the issue never became a reality.

This lunacy is not limited just to banking. At a previous law firm, I experienced some of the same warped thinking. One afternoon we received a memo...directive...edict from the grand high exalted mystic ruler (*Honeymooners* allusion) that our office was using precious supplies such as paperclips, tape, staples, and yellow sticky note pads at an alarming rate. Apparently the big boss man was having a difficult time financing his sixth Mercedes, so the time was ripe to trim the fat. Being relatively new at the firm, I figured that this memo was par for the course, as most of my fellow workers did not see it as absurd the way I did. The following day (and I mean literally the very next day), I noticed that King Tut (and his partners, the Tutettes), were not in the office. Not one of them. When I asked one of the secretaries about this matter, it was explained to me that this was the yearly trip for the higher-ups. She went on to advise me that once a year (sometimes twice a year), the Big Chief goes on vacation with the other partners in the firm (the Little Chiefs), including their entire families. He picks up the entire tab. Well, I thought, the Emperor's largesse must set him back a pretty penny, but he can sleep easy at night, safe in the knowledge that for an entire month I never used a single staple or paper-clip. If any documents needed to be fastened, I simply licked the documents until they were sufficiently moist and pressed them together. This method really saves on overhead. I had to drink more water than usual to keep my mouth watery, but it was bottled water purchased with my own money. I eschewed phone calls and instead screamed out the window hoping the other party could hear me. I also sent smoke signals. I used my sleeve for taking notes and wrote on a tissue brought from home if I needed to relay a message.

Don't get me wrong, I am a firm believer in the value of hard work and dedication to one's craft. But when I attend meeting after meeting with some brain-dead dolt executive who is trying to ascertain why the morale is so low in the office, I have to scratch my head. If they don't know the answer, they are either too stupid, too apathetic, or so far removed from the plight of the worker that they have lost sight of the big picture. The methods employed to handle and manage the grunts are shortsighted.

Nobody can quarrel with the desire to expand your business and turn a profit. That is as American as apple pie, baseball, and gossip. However, I truly believe that a little tweaking and in some cases a complete change in management style would serve to make the worker feel more appreciated and more a part of the team and the future of the organization.

In the end, the bosses might see an increase in production, efficiency, attitude, morale, and profit. A little kindness and respect goes a long way. It sounds corny, and it may not apply in every case, because some people are so lazy and miserable that nothing you give them would ever satisfy them. Cutting out some of the bullshit, being more open and frank, and creating a cooperative atmosphere would actually increase the bottom line. People respond more positively when they feel they are an important and contributing member of a team rather than in an atmosphere where your advancement is seen as my demise, and vice versa. We can learn to think differently. It may only hurt for a little while.

CHAPTER 7

FAMILY

AFTER WE ADD up all the pluses and minuses and calculate all the pros and cons, family is what it is all about. The family is where we acquire our strength, confidence, and values that we take with us when we leave our home each day to interact with society. As children, it is a building block toward adulthood and perhaps a template to use when we form families of our own later in life. Alex Haley said, "In every conceivable manner, the family is the link to our past, and the bridge to our future." Mother Teresa said, "What can you do to promote world peace? Go home and love your family."

We are even seeing a shift today in the business arena as the concept of trying to achieve a work–life balance is now seen as important. An unhappy life at home often creates an unhappy employee at the workplace. Many employers allow men to have a two-week parenting leave to assist their wife and newborn in the transition to the new edition of their lives. Being a father in today's world means more than just providing financial security, as more and more dads are actively involved in the child rearing process. They are not only at soccer games, school plays, and dentist appointments but they also participate in the maintenance and running of the household.

The advent of working moms has obviously forced many dads into domestic duties, but today's dads want to be family men as well as businessmen. Lee Iacocca said, "No matter what you've done for yourself or for humanity, if you can't look back on having given love and attention to your own family, what have you really accomplished?"

Dads spending more time with their children and participating more deeply in their lives fosters a stronger bond between dad and kids. Many nights my two daughters and I prepared dinner and sat at the island in our kitchen discussing subjects such as school, life, sports, movies, history, and people. To this day, I am not sure who learned more, them or me.

The expression *family values* is used a lot, but I'm sure it has different meanings to different people. I like to think of family values as the ideas, values, and principles that form the foundation of my family, allowing us to grow as a family and to create an environment wherein our different personalities can peacefully coexist, where a different opinion is treated with respect and where the whole is stronger than the sum of its parts.

Hopefully, my wife and I have cultivated a family unit where our children are loved, respected, cherished, and treated fairly (even when you want to strangle them with your bare hands). We believe they should be encouraged to dream, to find their path, and follow it with all their heart. Their high school principal once told me that along with encouraging the students to set lofty goals, study assiduously, and achieve high grades, he also emphasized the value of being a good person, a good human being, and a positive contributor to society. I love that notion.

Today's kids are constantly reminded how smart they are, how cute they are, and how special they are. Life is competitive, they are told, so get the kind of grades that will enable you to get into a good college and get a good job (as a parent of children in their twenties, my advice to parents of young children is that when you do their life plan, do it in pencil). You would be surprised how often the goals and paths change. Teaching your kids this lesson is a good idea. But don't shortchange them by teaching them only this lesson. Expand the lesson beyond what is merely best for just them to include how they could use their vast array of talents to help others, to inspire, or to just be there when someone needs them.

Just as I am sure how proud you feel about your children, I am extremely proud of the type of human beings that my daughters have become. My hope is that a lot of what they do today in a positive light got its origin in our family meetings, discussions, and battles. Reading together at night when they were young, cooking meals together, car trips, and vacations were the building blocks to forming the close relationship we all have now as they have grown into adults.

Many kids are confused and frightened today. You hear about it and read about it every day, and it breaks your heart. We can only hold out hope as parents that the lessons and values we taught our children and the love and support we provided them is a source of comfort during the dark days that we will all experience from time to time. My parents raised my sister and me with a strong belief in the importance of the family, and my wife and I have passed that along to our children. This does not mean that we are devoid of problems or that we don't fight or disagree from time to time (although how anyone can disagree with me boggles my mind). But our close-knit family unit provides us strength to deal with sadness and some bad times.

Don't ever stop encouraging your kids to be the best, to go to Harvard or Yale, to be a doctor, lawyer, or whatever they want to be. But also teach them how valued they are within the family structure, to respect themselves and others, to be tolerant of different views and lifestyles, to be loyal, to be compassionate, to be grateful, to be generous, to be honest with others as well as themselves. Believe me, our kids are capable of so much more than we were at their age, and of so much more than we think they are capable of. Stress the value of communication and of the notion that along with rights they also have responsibilities. Convey that they will be loved even when their opinion differs from yours, even when their vision for their life differs from yours. Tell them that the family unit is a safe haven when the outside world is cold, dark, and insensitive. Also let them know there are expectations regarding behavior and boundaries. Don't be afraid to get a little tough with them if their mouths are growing faster than their bodies (I just heard three upper crust yuppie latte drinking soccer moms faint onto the floor at this notion). Our kids are infinitely more resilient than we give them credit for, and it is a disservice to them to act in accordance with the idea that they are not capable of handling any disappointment or discipline, and foolish to believe that they can't handle the truth (who doesn't love Jack Nicholson).

Something that I think is extremely important, especially in today's technology-driven world, is that we create and value traditions. Traditions help a family feel close, develop a sense of uniqueness, and build memories. They also provide something that your children can build on and ultimately pass onto their kids. Like many families, we have many traditions that are important and significant to all of us. My favorite is one we started many years ago, and if my wife and I do anything to alter the tradition in any way, both daughters are ready with lawsuits. I am talking about the tree-lighting party, which we hold every year on the Saturday after Thanksgiving. This year will be our seventeenth party. The guest list includes my sister's family, my mom, dad, and mother in law, and any guests my children wish to include (my dogs participate as well). First we eat all the pizza, zeppole, and garlic knots we can shove into ourselves, along with any leftover Thanksgiving desserts. Then we play Christmas music and decorate the tree with ornaments (my sister's three kids do a lot of the ornament hanging and breaking). My nephew Nolan has broken more ornaments than Kim Kardashian has broken hearts. The point is that we have a great time and laugh a lot. My dad usually asks me around late July if we are having the tree-lighting party again this year. It has brought our family closer together, is something we all look forward to, and gives us a chance to begin the Christmas season before the utter madness of malls and debt rushes in. It has also served to be a source of comfort during some hard times.

I used to work with a guy who told me that every year on his birthday or on his sister's birthday, they get together with their entire family and eat pizza and drink champagne. They did this for years. They didn't even discuss it anymore, it was just known that this would be the plan for everyone's birthday. He described this tradition to me with a gleam in his eye, as if his family had invented a foolproof way of remaining close even as people move away or just get wrapped up in the busy nature and minutiae of life.

Earlier in this book I mentioned a few people who I admire for one reason or another. An individual I neglected to name but who I admire greatly is Lidia

Bastianich, host of a television program that you may have seen called *Lidia's Italy*. She is a master chef, author, and restaurateur as well. While I am aware that she is a world-renowned chef, and I have used many of her recipes (I love to cook), her television show is filled with warm stories of her childhood in Italy and her subsequent migration to America.

The meal and the family table are a vehicle to building a strong family unit and to pass ideals, values, and traditions from one generation to the next. Food doesn't have to be the vehicle, and being Italian is not a prerequisite. The most important idea is to have a sense of togetherness and closeness that cannot be separated by distance, to feel in touch with your roots and have a sense of stability. When I watch Lidia's show on a Saturday afternoon, besides getting hungry, I feel connected to my home and family. Her comfortable kitchen becomes my comfortable kitchen. I will jot down one of her recipes to be used during the holidays, at our Super Bowl party, or just for a special evening meal with my wife. The love she has for her family reminds me how lucky I am to have such a wonderful family.

In our busy and vast world, it is comforting to have a nice place to live with people there who care about us and love us. It seems that only in tragedy do we take stock of our lives, gain perspective, and tell ourselves to let the people around us who we love be made to feel loved. It shouldn't take horrific events such as the Newtown school shooting or the Boston Marathon bombings to remind us to kiss our kids goodnight and tell them we love them. That should be a daily occurrence. After both of these unspeakable tragedies, I called up both my daughters just to hear their voices. But tomorrow I promised myself that I would call up both of them to tell them I love them, not because of the fact that another parent unfortunately would not have this opportunity but rather for the simple reason that they deserve to hear those words from me every day.

CHAPTER 8

RANDOM THOUGHTS

AND OBSERVATIONS

COMMERCIALS

TRUTH BE TOLD, I hate commercials. I love the idea that while watching programs on Netflix or a DVD I can avoid seeing commercials, which serve to destroy the flow of the show. I also often watch a number of programs simultaneously, flipping back and forth like a crazy man, and I miss a lot of commercials this way. But when I am not on my toes, they slip a commercial in on me. I have noticed that a lot of companies are using the friendly neighborhood approach as their marketing strategy. The restaurant is your neighborhood place, the supermarket is your neighborhood grocer, and the pharmacy is your friendly neighborhood pharmacy. All of a sudden everyone has become Mr. Rogers, encouraging us to wait a few minutes as he changes into his sweater and sneakers. This may have a ring of truth to it in small town

America, but here on Long Island, and more so in New York City, the idea that an employee of a restaurant, supermarket, or pharmacy is taking the time out of their busy and unfulfilling day to create a dining atmosphere akin to your backyard barbeque, stopping you in the produce aisle to find out if you were satisfied with last week's peaches, or inquiring about your Aunt Ida's arthritis when you come in to pick up your seven hundredth prescription is absurd. The corporate big shots who love this idea and encourage the commercial to have this tone obviously don't work in the stores themselves. If they ever stopped in to visit, they would realize that the atmosphere is not exactly New Year's Eve in Times Square. This is not to say that the employees are rude and unprofessional, but the notion that these employees have an insatiable desire to serve and please the customer is a bit much. Let's reel it in a little bit. Tell us the food is fantastic, tell us the prices are low and the quality of the product is high, but stop with the nonsensical idea that the employee exists only to create a wonderful and exciting eating or shopping experience for the customer. Please also cease and desist in acting like dinner at your restaurant will remind me of Sunday dinner at Grandma's house or that shopping at your store will be like a meeting at the Raccoon Lodge (*Honeymooners* reference). Here's a flash: the public does not have that expectation. We want a good product at a fair price and a friendly and professional staff. Nothing or nobody has to be over the top.

Not a single person has ever come up to me and said, "Lou, I went to this great restaurant last night, the food was great and at good prices, but it lacked a Mardi Gras atmosphere so we refuse to go back, or, "Lou, we used to shop at this great supermarket, but the produce manager would not thump my melons," or "Lou, I just picked up some cough syrup at the pharmacy, but I would advise you never to patronize that establishment because the pharmacist did not inquire about the mosquito bite on my ring finger."

AMUSEMENT PARKS

I am fascinated by amusement parks (translation—I am scared to death and get lightheaded just staring up at the rides). What fascinates me is how many people go on these complicated, and utterly frightening rides without a care in the world. Often I see six- and seven-year-old kids getting off roller coasters with a big smile. When they see me as they exit the ride holding everyone's phones, jackets, and water bottles, they always assure me that the roller coaster was awesome, not at all scary, and that they are going on again with their four-year-old brother. I explain to these little punks (I mean little angels) that I have a condition wherein if I am suspended upside down, go backwards at two hundred miles per hour, or drop the equivalent of twenty-five stories, I could suffer a cardiac or neurological issue. It is at this point that the seven-year-old whispers into the ear of the six-year-old, and then they both explode in laughter. I guess you just can't discuss health with some people.

My further fascination lies in the fact that these same daredevils often fear things that seem innocuous. My older daughter, Deborah, for example, goes on every rollercoaster known to man. But if she sees a spider we have to call Dr. Phil to comfort her. Most of our society is afraid of change, commitment, public restrooms, the dark, the government, punk rock groups, heights, enclosed places, pit bulls, germs, their parents, their kids, and people who drive flat-bed trucks, yet here are all these people lined up for three hours to go on a rollercoaster ride that lasts twenty-five seconds, ready to endure high speeds, large drops, and going in multiple directions. Meanwhile, my wife and I had words at Disneyland when she was not sympathetic to my fear that she had raised the Dumbo ride more than five feet off the ground. I guess you just can't discuss physics with some people.

LOTTERIES

People are lined up at every convenience store and card store wherever I go purchasing Lotto tickets, Powerball tickets, Super Powerball tickets, Mega Powerball tickets, Win 3, Win 4, Win for Life, and every scratch-off game known to man. Since I am somewhat of a cynic, I never participate in these events. The only time I am coerced into participation is at the office, when we all chip in to win the big mamoo.

When the prize gets to be a certain amount, I get an e-mail from the director of fun and games at my office explaining that we should not be left out of this potential life-altering experience. Now, I am not sure what amount the prize has to get to for the social director to send around this compelling e-mail, but I think it is quite high, because in almost six years we have only played two or three times. I notice that other people do this as well. They play only when the amount gets into the hundred million area. Is this because when the prize money is at eighty-six million dollars it is not worth the buck or two investment? Or is it because after taxes the eighty-six million dollars will look more like forty-three million dollars, and who wants to be bothered with small change? I think the last time we played the big mamoo was around three hundred million dollars and the people here in New York absolutely lost their mind. People were playing around the clock. It was the only topic being discussed. Everyone at my job shared with me all the things they would do after they won, debating about coming back to work, maybe working part-time, taking time to stop and smell the roses, who they would share the money with, and who they would not share the money with. Deep thought was given to cars, vacations, vacation homes, and new girlfriends (the married guys waxed poetic on this subject). Much to our chagrin, the winning ticket was purchased at a store in Topeka, Kansas, or Cheyenne, Wyoming. As Maxwell Smart would say, "Missed it by *that* much."

I recently heard a radio show where the host threw out the idea that instead of shelling out hundreds of thousands of dollars to a college for a four-year degree, the parents should instead provide that amount to their child as an investment in their future. The child could use the money for college or as a nest egg to start a business or go into a line of work where college is not required. Apparently, according to some of the information I have learned from both print and electronic media, many kids are not staying for four years at one school, as they are bouncing from one school to another and one major to another, searching for the right fit. Others stop and start a few times, eventually graduating around their twenty-eighth birthday.

Some start off away and then come home and transfer to a school they can commute to from home. Others stop and never go back. All this serves to waste the money that many parents have sweated and toiled for since the birth of their child.

I don't know if the idea championed by the radio host is a good one, nor can I say with absolute certainty that college either is a valuable experience all must participate in or that college is a waste of money and is no longer a guarantee of future employment. However, what I can say is that the price of college is so exorbitant that it forces some students who have the grades but not the deep pockets go to an Ivy League school to go to a state school and forces some students to not attend college at all. In a competitive global wo economy, this is not the best way to help our students succeed, nor does it benefit our society.

A parent should not have to work two jobs and take out a second mortgage on their house to pay for a top education. I understand that there are many terrific state and smaller schools, but a student that is accepted to Harvard or Yale should be able to attend.

Every president in his State of the Union and Inauguration address seems to stress improving education and providing educational opportunities to deserving students as a way to ensure that our nation remains a global leader. Shouldn't we find a way to make this a reality for as many students as possible? This country wastes a lot of money on different things. There should be a way to assist students in attending the college of their choice or of encouraging universities to offer tuition commensurate with someone's ability to pay. In the end, we would all reap the benefits.

SPORTS

Discounting my family (and on occasion counting my family), sports is my love. I love the crack of the bat, a tight spiraling whistling toward the end zone, and the pretty arc of a three-point shot. Athletics are live and athletics are physical. You can practice all day, but you can never rehearse. The competition changes, the field of play changes, and the stakes change.

PERIPHERY

In a world filled with nepotism, incompetence, and prejudice, sports is the great equalizer. You can either hit a fastball or you can't. You can either make a tackle or you can't. You can either make a jump shot or you can't. It doesn't matter who your dad knows, how much money you have, or what your background or heritage is. If you prove that you can achieve in the athletic arena, they will find a place for you on their team.

I love to watch a baseball game on a warm summer night, a football game on a crisp autumn Sunday afternoon, and March Madness (in March of course). These games serve not only as a source of entertainment but also as a source of relaxation after a long day. They also afford me an opportunity to yell at the television for every bad coaching decision, blown call, and dropped pass.

Fans wear certain colors on game day, have routines that they are certain will affect the outcome of the game, and will sit in the same exact spot on the couch without movement for hours if their team is winning. It is amazing how much emphasis we place on the outcome of these games when they actually have very little to do with the state of our lives. But that is the great thing about sports. They can't pay your bills or put food on the table, but there is an indescribable feeling you experience when your team wins a big game, and a phenomenal high if they go on to win the championship. We feel connected to our favorite teams and our favorite players.

Some of our best memories come from our early days playing Little League baseball, Pop Warner football, or CYO basketball. I still participate in sports and love every minute of it (even though my routine on game day includes Advil, Ben Gay, and prayer).

Sports also helps us heal and come together in mind and spirit following national tragedies such as 9/11 and the Boston Marathon bombings. Sports is embedded in and is part and parcel of our society. For example, the 1989 San Francisco earthquake occurred during the World Series. A lot of the horrific images we saw came from the telecast of the game. In 1980, a group of college hockey players on the United States Olympic team shocked the world, beating the Russians on a Friday night and then defeating Finland on a Sunday morning to win the gold medal. The Miracle on Ice occurred with a hostage crisis, Russians in Afghanistan, soaring gas prices, long gas lines, and inflation as its backdrop. So how could a hockey game cure these ills? How can a baseball game where opposing players wear NYPD and FDNY hats, or where a Yankee fan wears a Red Sox cap, solve these problems? We know intellectually that it can't. But on a visceral level, it provides comfort, a distraction, or a brief respite from the devastation to allow us to feel something other than sorrow—an opportunity to feel alive again, even if for only a brief time until we revisit reality.

The great irony here is that sports makes us choose sides. My team against your team. My quarterback against your quarterback. Even my fantasy team against your fantasy team.

Debates that last generations are born out of sports. Mantle or Mays, Chamberlain or Russell, Lebron James or Michael Jordan, Joe Montana or Tom Brady (or Peyton Manning, to make my wife happy). We engage in arguments comparing Lombardi's Packers, Noll's Steelers, Walsh's Niners, Johnson's Cowboys, and Belichick's Patriots. Whether Cincinnati's Big Red Machine of the 1970s could have beaten the Yankees of the 1990s (we all know they could not). We have battles royale discussing the truly crucial questions facing mankind, like if Jordan's Bulls could have beaten Bird's Celtics, or Russell's Celtics, or Magic Johnson's Lakers.

Never have people felt so passionate about something that has so little effect on their lives. I have seen fans almost come to blows over their fandom. But most love good healthy competition and a well-played game (as long as my team emerges victorious). With all the side-taking in the world of sports, sports is at its most powerful and impactful in its ability to brings us closer together. We all witnessed this phenomenon recently following the Boston Marathon bombings. New York fans sang Neil Diamond's "Sweet Caroline" in tribute to their Boston brethren. Neil Diamond flew from Los Angeles to Boston unannounced to sing "Sweet Caroline" live at a Red Sox game. Boston Bruin fans sang the National Anthem with the zeal and energy deserving of the great city of Boston. It reminded me of Whitney Houston's beautiful rendition of the National Anthem at the Super Bowl in 1991 during the Gulf War. There is almost a patriotic feel to athletics. The Yankees and Red Sox can battle it out on the field, but we are all still Americans who despise getting screwed with and are here to support each other in times of national crisis.

Sports is a terrific tool in teaching its participants the value of hard work, discipline, teamwork, sportsmanship, winning with grace, losing with dignity, and of pulling together and putting egos and self-interest aside to achieve a common goal. It is the perfect metaphor for life itself.

CHAPTER 9

FAMOUS QUOTES

LOVE TO READ quotes. I never can understand how these quotes get memorialized or written down in the first place. Does someone hear a great thought, realize it has quote appeal, write it down, and then repeat it to as many people as possible until it becomes a quote? I am not even certain that a lot of these are really quotes. In any event, scattered through the book are some quotes that make me either laugh, think, wonder, or act.

" It's not that I am afraid to die, I just don't want to be there when it happens.

—*Woody Allen*

" Nothing I've ever done has given me more joys and rewards than being a father to my children.

—*Bill Cosby*

" Man is still the most extraordinary computer of all.

—*John F. Kennedy*

" Happiness is not something ready made. It comes from your own actions.

—*Dalai Lama*

" Freedom is not worth having if it does not include the freedom to make mistakes.

—*Mohandas ("Mahatma") Gandhi*

" If you want your children to keep their feet on the ground, put some responsibility on their shoulders.

—*Abigail ("Dear Abby") Van Buren*

" Do not let what you cannot do interfere with what you can do.

—*John Wooden (renown UCLA basketball coach)*

" It's kind of fun to do the impossible.

—*Walt Disney*

" It is Christmas in the heart that puts Christmas in the air.

—*W.T. Ellis*

" Really great people make you feel that you, too, can become great.

—*Mark Twain*

" If I were two-faced, would I be wearing this one?

—*Abraham Lincoln*

" Bigamy is having one wife too many. Monogamy is the same.

—*Oscar Wilde*

" There is no sincerer love than the love of food.
—*George Bernard Shaw*

" From the moment I picked your book up until I laid it down I was convulsed with laughter. Some day I intend reading it.

—*Groucho Marx*

" Show me a woman who doesn't feel guilty and I'll show you a man.

—*Erica Jong*

" I've learned that people will forget what you said, people will forget what you did, but people will never forget how you made them feel.

—*Maya Angelou*

" A narcissist is someone better looking than you are.

—*Gore Vidal*

" It has become appallingly obvious that our technology has exceeded our humanity.

—*Albert Einstein*

" I've had a wonderful time, but this wasn't it.
—*Groucho Marx*

" The true measure of a man is how he treats someone who can do him absolutely no good.

—*Samuel Johnson*

" A people that values its privileges above its principles soon loses both.

—*Dwight D. Eisenhower*

" I have not failed, I've just found 10,000 ways that won't work.

—*Thomas Edison*

" I'm living so far beyond my income that we may almost be said to be living apart.

—*E.E. Cummings*

" I find that the harder I work, the more luck I seem to have.

—*Thomas Jefferson*

" In the end, we will remember not the words of our enemies, but the silence of our friends.

—*Martin Luther King, Jr.*

" Don't stay in bed, unless you can make money in bed.

—*George Burns*

" Not everything that can be counted counts, and not everything that counts can be counted.

—*Albert Einstein*

" Any man who is under 30 and is not a liberal has no heart, and any man who is over 30 and is not a conservative has no brains.

—Sir Winston Churchill

" Find what makes your heart sing and create your own music.

—Mac Anderson (founder, Simple Truths)

" There is nothing like returning to a place that remains unchanged to find the ways in which you yourself have altered.

—Nelson Mandela

" What a gloomy thing, not to know the address of one's soul,

—Victor Hugo

CHAPTER 10

FAMOUS MOVIE LINES

WE ARE FASCINATED by lists. The top ten players, movies, songs, etc. You name it, we've got a list for it. The following are some movie lines that I think are outstanding and stand the test of time. To avoid arguing with myself, they are in no particular order, except for the last line, which is the greatest of all time:

" Attica, Attica.

> —*Al Pacino as Sonny Wortzik*
> DOG DAY AFTERNOON

" No wire hangers, ever.

> —*Faye Dunaway as Joan Crawford*
> MOMMIE DEAREST

" Keep your friends close, but your enemies closer.

> —*Al Pacino as Michael Corleone*
> THE GODFATHER II

"There's no crying in baseball.

—Tom Hanks as Jimmy Dugan
A LEAGUE OF THEIR OWN

"One morning I shot an elephant in my pajamas. How he got into my pajamas I don't know.

—Groucho Marx as Capt. Spaulding
ANIMAL CRACKERS

"Of all the gin joints in all the towns in all the world, she walks into mine.

—Humphrey Bogart as Rick Blaine
CASABLANCA

"Stella! Hey Stella!

—Marlon Brando as Stanley Kowalski
A STREETCAR NAMED DESIRE

"Well, nobody's perfect.

—Joe E. Brown as Osgood Fielding III
SOME LIKE IT HOT

"You've got to ask yourself one question: Do I feel lucky? Well do ya, punk?

—Clint Eastwood as Dirty Harry Callahan
DIRTY HARRY

"Louis, I think this is the beginning of a beautiful friendship.

—Humphrey Bogart as Rick Blaine
CASABLANCA

" You're gonna need a bigger boat.
> —*Roy Scheider as Martin Brody*
> JAWS

" You can't handle the truth.
> —*Jack Nicholson as Col. Jessup*
> A FEW GOOD MEN

" Made it, Ma. Top of the world.
> —*James Cagney as Arthur "Cody" Jarrett*
> WHITE HEAT

" Rosebud.
> —*Orson Welles as Charles Foster Kane*
> CITIZEN KANE

" They call me Mr. Tibbs.
> —*Sidney Poitier as Virgil Tibbs*
> IN THE HEAT OF THE NIGHT

" May the force be with you.
> —*Harrison Ford as Han Solo*
> STAR WARS

" Do, or do not. There is no "try."
> —*Frank Oz as Yoda*
> THE EMPIRE STRIKES BACK

" Why don't you come up sometime and see me.
> —*Mae West as Lady Lou*
> SHE DONE HIM WRONG

"You talkin' to me?

>—*Robert DeNiro as Travis Bickle*
>TAXI DRIVER

"I'm mad as hell, and I'm not going to take this anymore.

>—*Peter Finch as Howard Beale*
>NETWORK

"I'm gonna make him an offer he can't refuse.

>—*Marlon Brando as Vito Corleone*
>THE GODFATHER

"Toto, I've a feeing we're not in Kansas anymore.

>—*Judy Garland as Dorothy Gale*
>THE WIZARD OF OZ

"A census taker once tried to test me. I ate his liver with some fava beans and a nice Chianti.

>—*Anthony Hopkins as Hannibal Lecter*
>THE SILENCE OF THE LAMBS

"Frankly, my dear, I don't give a damn.

>—*Clark Gable as Rhett Butler*
>GONE WITH THE WIND

" You don't understand! I coulda had class. I coulda been a contender. I coulda been somebody, instead of a bum, which is what I am.

—Marlon Brando as Terry Malloy

ON THE WATERFRONT

" Say hello to my little friend.

—Al Pacino as Tony Montana

SCARFACE

CHAPTER 11

FINAL THOUGHTS
AND ACKNOWLEDGMENTS

I HAD A GREAT time writing this book. It was a fantastic (and sometimes frustrating) endeavor. I didn't realize how many thoughts and ideas would be altered in one way or another once they got down on paper, and sometimes even several days after a chapter was concluded. Bringing this book to life brought back a lot of fond memories (and at times painful memories). The process also made me think about people I hadn't thought of in years. Writing proved to be a cathartic experience and a wonderful journey of self-exploration. It was truly a labor of love.

I have many terrific people in my life, and without their support and encouragement this book would never have gotten off the runway. I am eternally grateful to them for their kind words and warm thoughts regarding the pursuit of my dream.

Many thanks to my mom and dad, Frances and Louis Bruno, both loving and supportive parents who passed on their work ethic, strong values, and love of family to my sister and me. The idea for this book was hatched in their home on Delaware Avenue. Thank you for always making me feel like a special son and thank you for the gift of life.

Many thanks to my mother in law, Sarah Gennardo, a great lady whose company I enjoyed from the minute we met. A son-in-law has never been treated with so much love and kindness. A strong and courageous woman who lost her son but never lost her ability to keep loving the rest of her family. Thank you for accepting me from day one.

Many thanks to my sister Sarah Doerrie, the world's best sister. She has always looked up to me and stuck up for me. One day we were playing games and sports in our parents' basement, and then somehow the next day she had a great husband and became a terrific mother to three wonderful children. Thank you for my niece and nephews and for that left turn in front of the Commack Public Library that I still can't make to this day.

Many thanks to my daughter Krista Nugent, a wonderful combination of the cerebral and the visceral, one of the most intelligent people that I have ever known and also one of the most caring. She shares my mischief, cynicism, and sense of humor (and of course my high intelligence). Thank you for being the kind of daughter a father could only hope for, and thank you for your love of art, love of animals, independent spirit, and honesty. I admire you more than words can express. I love you very much. I love watching *The Honeymooners* and *Columbo* with you. I love the fact that you still get a chuckle when I sign my name as Anakin Skywalker when I send you an e-mail, and I love our private jokes about Championship Chubs.

Many thanks to my daughter Deborah Nugent, a wonderful combination of the visceral and the cerebral, one of the most caring people I have ever known and also one of the most intelligent. She inspires me with the way in which she has handled tragedy and disappointments with such maturity, dignity, and kindness. Thank you for being the kind of daughter a father could only hope for, and thank you for your love of humanity, yoga, and animals and for your ability to make each person you interact with feel special and important. I love watching *M*A*S*H* and sports with you, and I love the fact that you let me tell you the same softball stories over and over again without ever letting me know that you have heard the story before.

Many thanks to my wife, Michelle Bruno, who encouraged the writing of this book from the beginning and kept me focused when doubt or laziness crept into my thought process. She is the most beautiful, intelligent, and ambitious person ever created, with a wonderful combination of business acumen, spiritual values, and love of family. She is my best friend and soul mate. We can love and laugh with the best of them, and we can disagree and argue with the best of them. I could never love, respect, or admire another human being as much as I do my wife. Michelle is an extremely successful banker who works more hours in a week than anyone should have to and still finds time to be a great mom, wife, daughter, daughter in law, aunt, and friend. Like my daughters, she provided great support both before and during the book writing process. I love you with all my heart and soul. I love the fact that you always know the next line that follows the line I give you from a mob movie, and I love the fact that we still get a kick out of saying, "This far and no farther."

Last, but not least, many thanks for reading this book. I wish you a good life filled with health and prosperity, and I encourage you to fulfill your dreams. Thanks again.

Louis Bruno

www.ingramcontent.com/pod-product-compliance
Lightning Source LLC
Chambersburg PA
CBHW071818020426
42331CB00007B/1524